"Stephanie has captured the heart of a grief journey and explains in simple terms what kind of response is needed from others. I would recommend this book to anyone with a grieving friend."

— PAMELA S. MICCA, M.Ed., LPC

"No longer will I avoid a bereaved friend out of the fear that I might say the wrong thing. No longer will I hug wounded people, promise to pray, and wonder what I'm supposed to do next. If someone you know is grieving, you need this book — and your grieving friend needs you."

— Angela E. Hunt, author of *The Awakening* and *Unspoken*

"From her own profound losses and various stages of grief, Stephanie shares unique insights that help the reader understand what thoughts and gestures are especially timely, meaningful, and sympathetic, as well as those that might seem right at the time, but, in fact, achieve a very undesired result."

— LINDA ISAACSON, RN, MSN, certified family nurse practitioner

"This is a long-overdue resource for those who are grieving, written by someone who truly lived it. The simple, practical suggestions for those who want to help are priceless."

— HELEN MARTIN, BSN, CHPN

"Once I started reading this book, I couldn't put it down. The advice is practical, and the journal entries are utterly compelling. As both a griever and a friend of grievers, I feel this book is a treasure."

— JANELLE CLARE SCHNEIDER, author

STEPHANIE GRACE WHITSON

HOW TO HELP
a GRIEVING
FRIEND

A CANDID GUIDE FOR THOSE WHO CARE

NAVPRESS®

BRINGING TRUTH TO LIFE

OUR GUARANTEE TO YOU

We believe so strongly in the message of our books that we are making this quality guarantee to you. If for any reason you are disappointed with the content of this book, return the title page to us with your name and address and we will refund to you the list price of the book. To help us serve you better, please briefly describe why you were disappointed. Mail your refund request to: NavPress, P.O. Box 35002, Colorado Springs, CO 80935.

The Navigators is an international Christian organization. Our mission is to reach, disciple, and equip people to know Christ and to make Him known through successive generations. We envision multitudes of diverse people in the United States and every other nation who have a passionate love for Christ, live a lifestyle of sharing Christ's love, and multiply spiritual laborers among those without Christ.

NavPress is the publishing ministry of The Navigators. NavPress publications help believers learn biblical truth and apply what they learn to their lives and ministries. Our mission is to stimulate spiritual formation among our readers.

ISBN 1-57683-677-0

Cover design by studiogearbox.com
Cover image by Photonica
Creative Team: Rachelle Gardner, Liz Heaney, Arvid Wallen, Kathy Mosier, Glynese Northam

Some of the anecdotal illustrations in this book are true to life and are included with the permission of the persons involved. All other illustrations are composites of real situations, and any resemblance to people living or dead is coincidental.

Published in association with the literary agency of Janet Kobobel Grant, Books & Such, 4788 Carissa Ave., Santa Rosa, CA 95405.

"After a While" © 1971 Veronica A. Shoffstall. Reprinted with permission.

Unless otherwise identified, all Scripture quotations in this publication are taken from the *King James Version* (KJV). Other versions used include: the *New American Standard Bible* (NASB), © The Lockman Foundation 1960, 1962, 1963, 1968, 1971, 1972, 1973, 1975, 1977, 1995 and *The New Testament in Modern English* (PH), J. B. Phillips Translator, © J. B. Phillips 1958, 1960, 1972, used by permission of Macmillan Publishing Company.

Whitson, Stephanie Grace.
  How to help a grieving friend : a candid guide for those who care /
Stephanie Grace Whitson.-- 1st ed.
    p. cm.
  ISBN 1-57683-677-0
  1. Church work with the bereaved. 2. Grief--Religious
aspects--Christianity. 3. Bereavement--Religious aspects--Christianity.
I. Title.
  BV4330.W47 2005
  259'.6--dc22

                    2004029522

Printed in Canada

2 3 4 5 6 7 8 9 10 / 09 08 07 06 05

FOR A FREE CATALOG OF NAVPRESS BOOKS & BIBLE STUDIES,
CALL 1-800-366-7788 (USA) OR 1-416-499-4615 (CANADA)

In loving memory of:

Kathy Sue Cole
1955–2000

B. Celest Higgins
1947–1996

James G. Swartz
1951–1998

Robert T. Whitson
1946–2001

"I am the resurrection and the life; he who believes in Me will live even if he dies, and everyone who lives and believes in Me will never die."

JOHN 11:25-26, NASB

Thank God, the Father of our Lord Jesus Christ, that
he is our Father and the source of all mercy and comfort.
For he gives us comfort in all our trials so that we in turn
may be able to give the same sort of strong sympathy to
others in their troubles that we receive from God. Indeed,
experience shows that the more we share in Christ's
immeasurable suffering the more we are able to give of his
encouragement. This means that if we experience trouble
it is for your comfort and spiritual protection; for if we
ourselves have been comforted we know how to encourage
you to endure patiently the same sort of troubles that we
ourselves endure. We are quite confident that if you have
to suffer troubles as we have done, then, like us, you will
find the comfort and encouragement of God.

2 CORINTHIANS 1:3-7, PH

contents

acknowledgments

Thank you, Brooke and JoAnna and Melissa and Matthew and Daniel and Nick, for sharing your experiences. Thank you for laughing, crying, creating, praying, and enlisting your own grief for the good of others by participating in this project.

Thank you, Janet, for believing and persevering and finding a home for the work of my heart.

Thank you, Pastor Gil and Marilyn, for listening and instructing and praying and helping me find my way to a new mission statement and a new life.

Thank you, Lauraine, for those late-night calls when you didn't let me get away with "everything is fine."

Thank you, Chris, for those hugs. And for not asking.

Thank you, Sis. The list would be too long.

Thank you to everyone who prayed me through the worst time in my life.

Thank you to the well-meaning but clueless for not staying away and for trying to help.

Thank you to Chuck and Kevin and all my brothers in Christ who helped me through financial quandaries and broken window cranks and siding dilemmas.

Thank you, Celestial Quilters. I'm so thankful God patched you into my life quilt.

Thank you, Daniel, for forgiving all my well-meaning but clueless attempts to comfort, for giving me tomorrow, for making me learn to ride a motorcycle, and for the heart. I'm keeping it.

INTRODUCTION

The world needs more people like you. The fact that you've opened this book shows that you care about others. Maybe you have a grieving friend you want to help. Perhaps you are the rare person who accepts death as part of life and wants to be prepared. Either way, the world needs more people like you.

When those we know and love lose someone *they* love, we all wonder, *What can I say? What should I do? How can I help?* Unfortunately, we usually don't know how to answer these questions. Because we don't want to say or do anything wrong, we feel awkward. We may even avoid the grieving person just when he or she needs us the most.

I know these things because I've done my share of avoidance and denial. But then came 1996. Since then, I've inhabited the other side of grief. With the loss of my best friend and both of my parents in 1996 and then my husband of twenty-seven years in 2001, I entered the world of the bereaved, and all the well-meaning but clueless things I had said and done in the past came back to haunt me.

This book is my attempt to use what I have learned "in the valley of the shadow of death" to help others avoid being well-meaning but clueless. People in grief and those who counsel the bereaved have read what follows and said, "Yes! Yes! I wish people knew that! If I'd had the guts, I'd have said just that!" Quick and easy to read, this little book will give you important insight into *how it feels* to experience a profound loss and then will offer you specific ideas on *how to help*.

The entries are arranged in three sections meant to approximate the early, middle, and late stages of the first two and a half years of my personal grief journey. I've named them Phase One: "I Can't," Phase Two: "I Must," and Phase Three: "I Can and I Will — by God's Grace." The entries are not exactly chronological because when they were written, I wasn't thinking of publication. I was trying to survive. I've done my best to put them into a logical sequence that accurately represents the seasons of my journey.

You will undoubtedly think that some of the more emotional entries are misplaced. *This can't be right,* you'll think. *She should have been past this stage.* Guess what? Grief doesn't happen in neat little stages. Please remember this when you help your friend. Just when we think we are making progress, grief has a way of rising up and slashing us right through the heart all over again. In fact,

I initially resisted the idea of any chronological arrangement in this project. But there is encouragement in the idea that, in spite of all the spiking and diving along the way, gradual progress over time does happen (assuming the grieving person works at it instead of going into prolonged denial). If I plotted my own journey on a graph, I would see many ebbs and flows. And, just as financial counselors look beyond the dips on market graphs to the long term and insist that investing is good for people over time, so, over the long haul, grief is mitigated. Friends who cosign for that long haul and stay around during the slides are rare treasures.

May God use these pages to bless your life and the life of your grieving friend. Please remember that every grief journey is as unique as the person experiencing it. What follows is not meant to be an all-inclusive manual, applicable in every case. Temper my suggestions with your personal knowledge of your grieving friend . . . and bathe everything you do and say in prayer. If you become aware of a mistake you've made, apologize.

This is important:

Don't stay away. *Don't* stop trying.

May the Lord who knows what is in the darkness give you wisdom to pierce it with love, and may He bless you for your willingness to minister to someone just when he or she needs you the most.

STEPHANIE GRACE WHITSON

PHASE ONE
"I can't"

I am weary with my groaning; all the night make I my bed to swim; I water my couch with my tears.

PSALM 6:6

HOW IT FEELS

I thought I'd want to be alone. I thought it would be overwhelming to share the day of death with anyone. I usually gain energy from being alone. So I thought once the hospice nurse and sheriff left and I'd talked with the funeral home . . . well, I thought I'd just want to wrap myself in a blanket and be alone.

But friends began to arrive. The kind of people who take charge, go get carryout, and fill the house with the laughter of good memories . . . among genuine tears.

I didn't think I'd want people around.

I was wrong.

HOW TO HELP

BRING KLEENEX

Paper plates, paper towels, napkins,
toilet paper . . . disposables
make a great gift right now.
You've saved me a trip to the store . . .
and made life at home easier.

USE PRESENT TENSE

If you slip up and mention my loved one
in the present tense, that's okay.
In my heart he or she is still very much alive.

PRETEND WITH ME

If I start to tell a story or talk about him or her,
don't get that "deer in the headlights" look.
Pretend he or she is still here.
As long as we remember, *my loved one is*.

HOW IT FEELS

If one more person quotes Romans 8:28 to me — or some other comfort cliché — I am going to SCREAM. I know Romans 8:28 by heart. I can read it in Greek. And French. It doesn't help. All I want is someone to listen to my pain. And maybe give me a hug. I haven't had a hug in a long, long time.

HOW TO HELP

DON'T APOLOGIZE FOR NOT KNOWING WHAT TO SAY
Chances are, there isn't anything you
can say that will really help.
Your hand on my shoulder, your hug, and
your presence mean a lot.

DON'T SPECULATE ABOUT THE UNKNOWABLE
If your faith teaches
that the dead don't see us and don't care about
life on earth "in light of eternity,"
keep it to yourself.
Saying that is the same thing
as saying he or she doesn't love me anymore.

LEAVE THE SELF-HELP BOOKS AT HOME
Unless you can say, "This helped me when my _____ died,"
just *don't* say it.

Delete Comfort Clichés

I *know* every cloud has a silver lining.

Remind me another time.

Hurt with me now.

HOW IT FEELS

His rocking. I wish I could dispel the image from my mind.

His starving frame with prominent hip bones and cavernous waist poised on the edge of the bed, rocking with all his might; his hand reaching out, repeatedly falling off the handle of the bedside commode. His hands . . . the hands I always loved so much look like claws, enlarged by the fact that his arms have shrunk to nothing, and they shake like an old man's. Part of him has already departed. This man, the one poised on the edge of the bed and the edge of eternity, is but a shell of the man I loved. When I finally make him listen and understand, he stops. He lies back down. I call the nurse. And he gives up one more piece of his dignity.

It was — and is — a terrible moment. For both of us.

I wish I didn't remember the rocking.

HOW TO HELP

IF YOU TELL ME, "CALL ANYTIME," MEAN IT
Your phone could ring at 3:00 AM because
I'm having nightmares.
If you don't really want me to call anytime,
please . . . don't say it.

❧

LET ME BE ANGRY
It may not make any sense at all,
but some days I'm just mad —
at people who still have what I've lost,
at people who are too nice,
at God.
Just let me vent.

❧

Understand

I've faced horrors that you can't imagine
and I can't bear to relive.
Understand this . . . and be gentle.
Please don't ask for medical details.
If I want to talk about them, I will.

HOW IT FeeLS

I didn't expect listening to music to be so hard. I still can't bear the lyrics promising, "I will be here." They make me angry. Bob promised to be here. But he's not. I know the anger is irrational. Still, I feel it. And then the anger turns to guilt. It's not fair to be angry. He fought for life for as long as he could.

I've had to turn off the road so I can do my own wailing after hearing a singer wail, "What'll I do without you?" What, indeed, *will* I do?

I drive around town in silence now because I'm tired of being surprised by uncontrollable emotions brought on by the words of a song.

I'll know I'm healing when I can listen to the radio again.

HOW TO HELP

CHANGE THE MUSIC

Love songs hurt grieving spouses.

Family songs hurt grieving children.

Friendship songs hurt grieving friends.

BEWARE OF MOVIES

Think before you invite my kids or me.

Is the movie about what we just went through?

HOW IT FEELS

Joni shoveled the walk today. I looked out on the world of white, and there she was, a woman from my church, wielding a shovel along the sidewalk. My house is on a corner lot. I have a *lot* of sidewalk.

"Joni," I called out. "You don't have to do that."

"I wanted to do . . . something," she said, her voice breaking. "Please just let me do this."

I have a snowblower. Joni doesn't know that. She also doesn't know I have no idea how to run it. He always did that.

I went back inside and started to cry — angry tears — because he can't do it, because I don't know how to run the snowblower, because I am needy. But the tears changed, eventually, to tears of gratitude for a God who sends a sister in Christ to shovel snow.

HOW TO HELP

Offer to Do Things

I'm drowning in to-do lists
I don't have the energy for.
Help me figure out my taxes.
Take my daughter to shop for school clothes.
Prune *her* roses.
Mow *his* lawn.
Clean the refrigerator.
Repair the broken window.
Just do it.

Be Willing to Do What I Need You to Do — Not What You *Think* I Need You to Do

Maybe the broken window crank reminds me of him.
I may not want it fixed right now.
Maybe the ragged wreath on the front door reminds me of her.
I may not want it "freshened up."
Every grief has its own shape.
Listen to me and accept *my* journey.
If you aren't sure, ask me.

And please *do* take no for an answer
without requiring an explanation.

≈

Don't Expect a "Thank You" Card
I just don't have the energy to
observe social graces right now.
I am grateful.
Just know it.

HOW IT FEELS

It's just God and me now. He is supposed to be enough. God forgive me for saying it, but sometimes "God and me" feels like just me. No arms, no voice, no music. Just darkness. I spent twenty-seven years building a life that was swept away, not by a tornado or a hurricane, but by one breath that didn't come. No arms. No voice. No music. No future. Dear God . . . what *were* you thinking?!

HOW TO HELP

Bypass Sympathy Cards That Say,
"Rejoicing with You"

I'm not rejoicing. I feel awful.
And now there's something *else* wrong.
Even my faith is in trouble
if I should be rejoicing.
Because I can't.

Let Me Say the Words
I'm *shattered*.
I'm *sad*.
I'm *lonely*.
I'm *terrified*.
Defining my feelings
is the beginning of coping.
Don't be frightened by the words.
Saying them is part of my healing.

Be Patient

I am making my way in a world
where my primary connection
to reality is gone.
Don't tell me I should "get over it" and "move on."
As soon as I'm ready, I will.
But *your* timetable is irrelevant to
my reality.

HOW IT FEELS

I can't drive south on 56th Street. That's the best way home. It is also the way I drove home the morning he died. It's crazy and illogical. But I can't drive south on 56th Street anymore.

It's a lovely evening — around sunset with perfect fall weather. I turn onto South Street and head west, and within a few blocks of my destination, I have to pull over and cry. This is the first time I've come this way since my friend died. I didn't expect the drive to be a problem. I didn't even think about it. But here I sit, leaning over the steering wheel, crying.

HOW TO HELP

TELL ME I'M OKAY
Grief makes people a little crazy.
Remind me that I shouldn't be expected
to behave "like my old self."
It's good to know I'm *not*
going crazy — at least not permanently.

ACCEPT MY NEW QUIRKS
If I'm reluctant, don't push it.
Grief changes people — permanently.
I may never be "my old self" again.
But I just might be a *better* self
if you'll give me some time.

HOW IT FEELS

I cannot listen to the sermon today. I do not care about parsing verbs or premillennialism. I *know* my hope is in the future. My life is on autopilot while I wait for and anticipate reunion and eternity. Certainly I am glad to know that someday God will wipe away all tears, for I have cried enough. I should be content with "the everlasting arms" — but I am not. If I say, "Not my will but thine be done" often enough, will I eventually stop wanting him back and accept his departure as God's will and therefore as ultimate good? My heart is broken, my world has been destroyed . . . and the lesson today is on prophecy. I don't know how I am going to get through the next five minutes. I don't *care* about what will happen during the seven-year Tribulation.

HOW TO HELP

INVITE ME TO SIT WITH YOU

Church is one of the hardest places to be.

Sitting alone in that pew is devastating.

All the expressions of care are overwhelming.

Shelter me.

Let me hide out next to you.

HOW IT FeeLS

It's Mother's Day. The card has a silly picture of a horse on it. Not your typical Mother's Day sentiment. On the front of the card my son has written the first line from a joke his dad used to tell, with the punch line inside.

I just received my favorite Mother's Day card of all time. A happy memory.

HOW TO HELP

SHARE THE LAUGHTER
Tell me something funny
you remember about my loved one.
Laughter really *is* the best medicine.

SEND US PICTURES
If you have photos of all of us together,
share them.
They might be the only ones we'll have.
And they bring back happy memories.
Even if the pictures make us cry,
we want them.

DON'T SAY,
"YOU NEED TO MAKE NEW MEMORIES"
Right now, I need to remember
the old ones.

HOW IT FeeLS

"We're having a family picnic," the voice on the other end of the line says, "and we're taking family photos. Now, I know that will be hard for you, but we'll all just have a good cry and get on with it."

Uh . . . excuse me? No. We won't "just have a good cry." We already do enough crying, and we're not ready to "get on with it."

HOW TO HELP

Skip Inviting Our Family to Organized Family Events for a While

They are just too hard.

We don't feel like a family anymore.

Accept No for an Answer

It's exhausting pretending to be happy
in a group so I don't depress
everyone around me.
If I say no, it doesn't mean I don't want your friendship.
It just means I'm too tired to hang out right now.

HOW IT FEELS

"I'm so sorry," he says and puts a hand on my shoulder. "I didn't mean to make you cry."

I can't quite explain it standing there in the hallway at church, but the tears aren't all sorrow. Some of them are a quiet, comforting kind of joyful angst because this man has just stopped to tell me — after all these months since my beloved died — how much he is missed.

See . . . you're not the only one.

Sweet comfort, to know I'm not the only one. Others miss him too.

HOW TO HELP

SAY THE NAME

Nothing hurts worse than thinking
everyone else has forgotten him or her.
It's comforting to know that someone remembers,
even if it makes me cry.

REMEMBER THE DATES

Valentine's Day, my birthday,
his or her birthday, our anniversary
are going to be awful this year.
And then there is the new one:
Death Day.
You can't change the awfulness,
but knowing that you remember
makes me feel less alone.

Visit the Cemetery

Leave a note, a flower, or anything
that seems appropriate.
It helps to find evidence that others remember too
and still care enough to go out of their way to show it.

HOW IT FEELS

Sometimes it just seems like too much. Thanksgiving followed by our anniversary followed by Christmas followed by New Year's Eve followed by football bowl games followed by the Super Bowl followed by my birthday followed by that day when, only a year ago, I whispered in his ear that when he saw Jesus, he should go. I urged him out of his body and into . . . what, exactly, I don't know. I don't know where he is . . . or what form a person takes after the soul leaves the body. And yet I am so convinced he still is. I imagine him walking streets of gold to visit friends and family who have "gone on before." And I picture him watching us from above at critical moments of our lives.

I have been doing very well of late, really. I even sat alone at church on Sunday night and made it through. I'm "getting on." It's expected, of course, and I've always been a person who seeks to please others. So I discuss redecorating my office, as if the colors of the walls matter to me. I decorate for Christmas, as if I care that the house shows the world that even though death comes, we still believe. I still *do* believe. But I don't care if the house is decorated for the holidays. I did it today, and the satisfaction came from knowing how much he loved decorating for Christmas. *He would be pleased*, I tell myself. In that knowledge there is some comfort, I suppose.

I know I matter to God and my family and a few friends. I know I serve a purpose in the world. Or else I wouldn't be here.

But still, the days pass and hold little interest for me.

I am going through the motions of reality. I am not really connected to it.

The Christmas lights are beautiful. But they don't matter.

My next book will be out soon. It doesn't matter.

Nothing matters, really, because I have lost the one person in this world who was "my only one," who shared all my secrets and loved me anyway.

There is a great divide between us. One of earth when I visit the cemetery and one of space everywhere else.

We are only one heartbeat away from one another.

When, I wonder, will that heartbeat of time be crossed?

And what am I to do until then?

The next thing.

I do the next thing.

I do it well most of the time.

I don't think anyone suspects how little it matters to me.

HOW TO HELP

SEND FLOWERS — LATER
It takes a while for the permanency
of my loss to sink in.
I will probably need signs of your caring
even more later.

HOW IT FEELS

I'm drowning in "to-do's" like choosing siding/fence and washing windows and managing lawn care and deadheading flowers and mulching flowers and programming sprinklers and driving the old car paying bills filing moving the file cabinet setting up the bed and dresser painting inside upholstering the last chair hanging drapes in the library taking flowers to the grave writing answering fan mail arranging cell phone for teenager quilting for daughter cleaning inside sorting garage calling lawyer getting haircuts working out mending making meals scrubbing kitchen floor shampooing carpet attending volleyball games baseball games voice lessons guitar lessons church Bible study volleyball practice baseball practice teaching her to drive arranging direct deposit trimming dog's nails finishing dog run feeding and spraying roses killing grass in berms deciding what to plant on west side of house and planting it getting bird houses hung right keeping lawn mowed reading paper setting up database creating website waxing and vacuuming car sending "thank you" notes canceling newspaper changing house exterior lights planting top row of perennial bed calling for doctor checkups planning summer reading serving in Vacation Bible School attending CBA/*chi libris*/Mark's wedding/AQS volunteering at IQSC writing family staying in touch and all of this when none of this is what I want to do which is run away and be someone else for a while. My world was defined by him and now he is gone and everything is unraveling.

HOW TO HELP

PROVIDE CHILD CARE
I'm overwhelmed with the basics of life.
If I need a break, you can be certain the children do too.
Take them away from the chaos.
Give us all a break.

༚

BE SPECIFIC
"Call me anytime" has no meaning.
"I can run errands for you from 10:00 AM to noon on Saturday"
means you mean it.

༚

WAIT
If I need a life coach, you are the first one I will call.
No, really . . . the very first one.
Stay by the phone and wait for my call.

HOW IT FEELS

Not Being There is what I did last year. I was not There because my Here felt too overwhelming for me to contemplate anything else. In 2000, the world was supposed to come to an end. And though the world would survive, my life would not. My husband was dying.

Helping him die took all my energy. I was Here for him and our four children. I was not There for my friends. Most of them understood. One did not. One told me that while he was going through the worst time of his life, I was a failure as a friend. His life had been awful, he said, and I was not There for him.

I cannot apologize for my failure. If I lived it over again, I could do no better. It was my year of Not Being There for my friends. But I was Here for my husband. I did a good job of taking care of him. I did a good job of nursing and loving him, and when the space between his breaths became all space and no breathing, I was at peace . . . without regret. What a gift. Could I relive that year, I would still choose Being Here for my husband and Not Being There for a stressed friend.

I have wanted to scream the reality of what I went through to those who just don't seem to get it. I have wanted to yell about catheters and skeletal bodies, about feeding nightmares and listening all night to labored breathing. Maybe it would help them understand the why of my Not Being There.

But I don't want to reduce my beloved's valiant struggle to a contest of Who Had It Worse. He deserves better. So do I.

I wasn't There. My job was Here.

Please try to understand.

HOW TO HELP

CHOOSE ANOTHER COUNSELOR
I simply cannot bear your burdens right now.
I'm concentrating on breathing and
on getting out of bed in the morning.

COUNT YOUR BLESSINGS
Hearing you complain about your family
hurts me. It really, really hurts.
I'd kill to have my loved one
back right now.
Whine to someone else.

OVERLOOK MY FAILURES
I really, really can't help it.

PHASE TWO
"I MUST"

Save me, O God; for the waters are come in unto my soul. I sink in deep mire, where there is no standing: I am come into deep waters, where the floods overflow me. I am weary of my crying: my throat is dried: mine eyes fail while I wait for my God.

PSALM 69:1-3

HOW IT FeeLS

We always said cancer was in our lives but we would not let it be our lives. His absence is in my life . . . and, God help me, it *is* my life. For everywhere, in everything, I feel his absence.

When I wake, he is not there.

When I rise, he is not there.

When I work, he is not there.

No phone rings to share a problem. No hands reach out to hold me. No voice soothes my fear. No lips kiss away my anger. No laughter joins mine. No arms hold me.

When I go to bed, he is not there.

When the alarm goes off, another day begins, and the same absence, the same sadness, the same aloneness reigns over everything.

HOW TO HELP

DON'T ASK IF THINGS ARE
"BACK TO NORMAL"

Normal just isn't a word that describes any aspect
of my life right now. My reference point for
normal has been ripped away.
In time, I'll get a new definition.
But right now, I don't know what *normal* means.

OFFER TO INCLUDE MY CHILDREN
IN YOUR FAMILY OUTINGS

For us, going out is painful
because of The Empty Chair.
When you include my children in your events,
you bring a sense of normalcy to their lives,
which is something I can't do right now
because I'm not ready to go out.

Call Me from Work

Everything about every day
will be harder for a while.
Hearing your voice in the middle of the lonely day
might help.

HOW IT FeeLS

This past week the worst part hit me. He was the only person in the entire universe to whom I was "his only one." No one else in all of creation feels this way about me. Not even God. God loves everyone. Christ died for everyone. But Bob loved *only* me. And for the first time in nearly thirty years, I have no one who loves me that way. I am no one's "only one."

A friend heard me say this, but she didn't get it. She reworded what I said. She said that what I really missed was "having someone to love." No . . . what I miss is being loved. What I miss is exactly what I said. What I miss is the knowledge that someone in the world feels about me the way no one else in the universe ever has. I will never again see his eyes light up just because I walked into a room. I will never again know the exquisite joy of sharing intimate secrets and memories and delights with only him — memories that no one else can share or understand or delight in. Those wonderful, awesome experiences died with my husband.

That is what I miss. That is the gaping hole in my life that cannot be filled.

HOW TO HELP

DON'T EDIT WHAT I SAY
It's not about making it easier for you to hear.
It's about letting me say what I mean.
At the moment you hear it,
I *do* mean what I say.

༼༽

TELL ME TO WRITE A BOOK
Give me a blank book and a pen and tell me to write —
to God about the things I'm afraid to verbalize,
to the one I miss about exactly what I miss,
to my well-meaning but clueless friends about
how much they hurt me.
The book can provide a place to put the pain.
By putting it there, I begin to contain it.
If it is there, I can walk away from it.

HOW IT FEELS

A wedding. I slip into a pew where I think I will be all right — toward the back, just in case I have to leave. Four people slide into the pew in front of me. They haven't seen me in months.

One turns around, sympathy dripping from her down-turned mouth and sad eyes. "Hello. How *are* you?"

Uh-oh. I hate it when people emphasize the second word of that question.

"Great." That's all I say. And I mean it. I just returned from an inspiring business trip, coming home to no husband and a life I never wanted, and it wasn't horrible. Last time it was. I'm making progress.

"Really?" She can't quite believe my answer.

"Yes. I'm doing well. Really." I am trying to tell her, *Let it go. I do not want to go where you are going.*

But she can't let it go. Her need to show concern prevents her from seeing my need to talk about the good things in life. "How long has it been now?"

I sigh inwardly. "Six months."

"Really? I had no idea it had been that long."

Now, this is really helpful. She has been so caught up in her own life . . . and time just flies when we're having fun, doesn't it?

I don't help her out of her dilemma. I don't offer to change the subject, either. I tried that with the first word out of my mouth. She didn't follow my lead.

I sit quietly, wondering what she's going to say next. She has nothing to say. So, awkwardly, she smiles, nods, and turns back around.

I move to another pew to hide out near a friend who understands.

Later, I pondered the incident. Why on earth would a casual acquaintance think I would want to discuss with her the worst thing that has ever happened to me? Doesn't she realize forcing me to focus my attention on the death of my husband is not a good idea at a wedding?

HOW TO HELP

**IF YOU HAVEN'T SEEN ME FOR A WHILE,
DON'T MAKE ME SLOG THROUGH RECENT WEEKS
TO UPDATE YOU**

The hand on the arm, the Compassionate Expression,
the overemphasized, "How *are* you?"
in the grocery store or at the mall
make me want to run the other way.

ACCEPT YOUR ROLE IN MY LIFE

Don't designate yourself as The One
I spill my guts to.
And don't be offended if you aren't
the person I choose.
Just accept where I am.
Quietly.

Talk About the Weather

I don't want to give a report every time I see you.
Sometimes I'd like to pretend it never happened.
So talk about the weather.
If I need to talk about something else,
you'll probably know after a sentence or two.

HOW IT FEELS

"Well, you *know*," the voice on the other end of the line says, "if you even *think* about dating for at least a year and a half, we are going to *kill* you."

I reassure the voice and hang up a few minutes later, amazed at the audacity of the caller. How dare someone judge me so easily, assign a time to my grieving, and assume the position of authority as if I need permission? And just how do friends and acquaintances arrive at the one-and-a-half-year requirement? Besides, can't they see that my loneliness and desire for companionship honor my deceased partner? Our marriage was so wonderful, so rich, that I long to be married again.

I, who thought I would never, ever engage in relationship building again, have begun to think perhaps, just perhaps, with the right person it would be worth the effort. Perhaps life is not too short after all, and I am not too old to love again.

I am not certain I want to wait as long as a year. What is to be gained by a year of loneliness and tears?

I am not certain of any of this. And yet I don't need people telling me there is some magic number after which I will be "ready." I resent their inserting themselves into this, the most intimate part of my life, uninvited and with answers to questions I am not asking.

Tonight my daughter asks me if I would ever consider dating or marrying someone again. I am startled by the question because in the past few days, I have been thinking a lot about dating and marrying again. Seeing my shocked look, she instantly apologizes and retracts her question. I tell her that she is not to bring up the subject again. I am enraged at myself. Are my thoughts a betrayal of my mate? No. Wanting another love means the first one was wonderful. Didn't I just write that in my journal? *Betrayal. Compliment.* Which is it?

My eldest daughter lets me cry on her shoulder and tells me that I don't need to feel guilty, that my children know I adored their father. This is all very normal, I have been told — all these emotions and thoughts whirling and swirling around me, keeping me from knowing even how to pray. There is something absurd about being the topic of conversation among people who are watching. I will admit to liking the idea of once again being in love. And I will also admit to wishing my "only one" were back here in my life, healthy and whole and saving me from all these muddled feelings.

HOW TO HELP

IF I TALK ABOUT DATING,
BE SUPPORTIVE

Wanting another relationship is a tribute to my mate.

I want what we had again.

It doesn't mean I didn't love him.

It means I don't want to live without love.

DON'T ASK IF OR WHEN
I'M GOING TO DATE

If I'm not ready, I'll feel like you're rushing me.

If I am ready, you'll know.

Either way, just leave this subject alone —

unless I initiate it.

HOW IT FeeLS

Life goes on. That's the trouble. Things swirl around me, but nothing — not one single thing — is the same or what I expected. From my getting up to my lying down, every moment brings a reminder that my life has been shattered.

I wake up each morning to an empty half of the bed — and silence. No sounds of another living person getting ready for work. No competition for the bathroom. No steamed-up mirror. No need for the double sink. No beard stubble in the sink. No need for two towel bars. Only my bottle of shampoo in the shower. Half-empty drawers and cupboards and closets.

No need to dress to please him anymore, although I still think about what he would like and feel guilty if I venture outside his lines.

No need to coordinate my schedule with another person. No one will be inconvenienced if I lunch at eleven or not at all.

At work, I can't pick up the phone just to call and hear his voice or tell him I love him. I won't ever meet him for lunch again and feel that thrill when the handsome man in the corner booth has eyes for only me. No worrying over what I eat or how I'm shaped. No one to care. No suits to be picked up at the cleaners after work.

No need to arrange my day around a 5:30 PM homecoming that sets the tone for the rest of the evening. One less place setting and serving at supper. I cook whatever I like. His likes and dislikes, around which I planned meals for twenty-seven years, no longer matter. Sometimes I don't even remember how *I* liked things. The condition of the house isn't as important, either. The kids don't notice, and I don't have company because it makes his absence more evident.

And then come the evenings. Awful, awful evenings. Worse weekends. I plan and go and do, but none of it seems right somehow. I am so relieved when the children are occupied elsewhere because then I don't have to be an entertainment committee. I don't mind chauffeuring, but participating is such a chore.

I can watch what I want on television and skip the sports. No one flips the channels. No one challenges where I want to sit. Only *my* books and papers and projects clutter the bedroom now.

At bedtime there's no one to hint that it's getting late. I have no thought of which pajamas or lingerie to wear — or not wear. It doesn't matter. All I do in my bed now is sleep. Nothing else is going to happen. How I hate that. I set the alarm for when I need to rise. And if I wake in the night from a bad dream, I don't have to worry about bothering anyone else's sleep. I can get up, turn on the lights, do whatever. It's up to me to deal with my fears and nightmares. There's no one to put his arms around me and tell me not to be afraid, that he loves me.

I never thought I would have to live the nightmare of Not Being Loved. But now I do live it every day, and there will be no waking up from it until the day I die. He doesn't love me anymore, and for that I am angry. How *could* he just go and leave me like this?

HOW TO HELP

BE PATIENT
I'm muddling around in a world without rules,
doing a job without a job description.
It may take me longer than the usual probation period
to get this life figured out.

WORRY LESS
If I suddenly show up with a pierced ear or a tattoo or a Harley,
don't make too much of it.
It was probably something I have always wanted to do and just
needed to do now
while I have an excuse to be a little crazy.

FORGIVE ME
The chances are very good that nothing I say or do right now
has anything on earth to do with *you*.
So don't let any of it offend you.

HOW IT FEELS

I have been alone for ten months now. Longer, really. In those last months, he slowly withdrew. He was drawing nearer to heaven, as he should have been. But the watching and the loss were so hard. It hurt to see the fire in his eyes that meant desire for me die. I longed for his touch — for him to just hold me — but he could no longer muster the energy or interest. I sat on the floor beside the bed, weeping while he stroked my hair. He pitied me. He didn't *want* me anymore. I remember running into another room, lying facedown on the carpet, and screaming with despair. It shocked him. It relieved me. For a while.

HOW TO HELP

IF YOU HUGGED ME BEFORE, HUG ME NOW;
IF YOU DIDN'T HUG ME BEFORE, HUG ME NOW

Babies who are not held die.

They experience a "failure to thrive."

I have enough to deal with just now.

Don't add sensory deprivation to my list.

HOW IT FEELS

Of course I'll go on. What choice do I have? To do anything else would be a complete denial of everything I've said I believe all these years. And then there are the children. I can't leave them, although they need me less and less. Still, I hope in some small way to model for them survival after the worst.

But, oh, my heart. How it aches. Even after ten months and a few hours, I feel the physical hurt of the loss, the aloneness. I never expect it to sneak up on me, unbidden like it does. Even after I've had good days when I laughed and was glad to be alive, I can still feel this secret hurt. I am an actress with a part to play. And I will play it well. Already I am receiving rave reviews.

I don't feel despair most of the time now. It's a duller, ever-present sense that I will never, ever be happy again. Most of the time I can cope with it pretty well. I beat it back into submission and keep it from nibbling at the edges of the day's to-do list. I have managed, I think, to sufficiently hide the presence of this gaping hole in my heart so that no one suspects it even exists anymore. I think most people see me as doing very well and being very courageous and all the other sickening phrases people use to describe this state of nonbeing called bereavement.

HOW TO HELP

BE SUSPICIOUS OF MY SMILES
I learned very quickly to hide
my misery so I won't drag other people down.
Don't always believe my mask.

༄

DON'T TELL ME
YOU KNOW HOW I FEEL

You don't.

༄

ACCEPT MY TEARS
Don't be embarrassed when I cry.
Tears are healing.
They must be shed.
Crying alone hurts worse.

HOW IT FeeLS

"She'll be fine." That's what everyone said about me after my husband died. "She's a strong woman," they said. "Amazing faith. Great example. And it isn't like his death was a surprise. They'd known for years it wasn't curable. She told me herself they realized last summer he wasn't going to get better. They had time. Nothing left unsaid. He even planned his own funeral. Terrific guy. Left a tremendous legacy."

So, after the funeral and a few perfunctory cards and prayers, they went on with their lives. Most never, ever suspected the woman they all admired was drowning in a sea of grief.

I couldn't tell them. I was too busy trying not to sink to even cry out for help. Treading water took all my energy. Keeping my head above the waves of chores and decisions and single parenting left me no energy and little time for acknowledging and dealing with my emotions.

"How are you doing?" they ask from time to time. I don't know how to answer that question. I've stopped trying.

"Fine. I'm doing fine." I can see the relief in their eyes when I answer that way. They have done their Christian duty by me, and I have not added to their burdens of life with a burden of guilt. I have saved them from the details of a life they can't understand — and a reality they might have to face themselves someday. And they really, really do *not* want to go there.

So I'm fine. Really. Just fine.

I will learn to maintain the lawn mower. I will learn to manage the retirement funds. I will follow his diagram and instructions and successfully gear up the underground sprinklers for another season. I will see to it that our youngest son has companionship and input from Christian men.

But oh, dear Lord, there is nothing I will ever be able to do to fill the void in my life caused by the absence of my one and only best beloved.

I will survive. I will cope. Others will look at me and admire me. They will call me "a rock." And they will never, ever know that beneath the strength and the coping is a black hole of sadness so great I fear even God Himself cannot fill it. That is very near blasphemy, I know. I pray He will forgive me for thinking it. Perhaps in the thinking and acknowledging I will know some small victory over my fear.

How to Help

Don't Tell Me How to Feel

I *know* that my loved one "is in a better place."

But I am *here*, and it hurts.

Accept my pain.

Don't tell me not to feel it.

Remember

Two months, six months, a year after my loss,

I am still facing new hurts.

A note or an e-mail

that tells me you know

means a lot.

Instead of Giving Me Stuff, Give Me *You*

My freezer is full of casseroles.

My mailbox is full of cards.

I need someone to cry with.

PHASE THREE
"I CAN AND I WILL — BY GOD'S GRACE"

"Behold, I have refined thee, but not with silver; I have chosen thee in the furnace of affliction."

ISAIAH 48:10

Unless thy law had been my delights, I should then have perished in mine affliction.

PSALM 119:92

Quicken me after thy lovingkindness; so shall I keep the testimony of thy mouth.

PSALM 119:88

Thou art my hiding place and my shield.

PSALM 119:114

HOW IT FEELS

I may have turned a corner. Just for a flicker of a moment today, I felt as if I am going to be all right without you. I have been struggling *not* to have my entire existence defined by your death-day, even though it was probably the most significant event of my life, aside from my salvation and our marriage. It has reigned over every waking moment of every day since then. But I'm not certain it has borne the fruit it should. I've been letting it draw me inward, away from people. I've been letting it occupy my thoughts and prayers, which have been largely about me for a long time.

Surely that is not what God intended to accomplish in my life when He took you home. It's easy to see how it was good for you. I've begun to call that day your "graduation day." The question is, how can it be made good for me? How can it make me of more use to the Lord? I'm not certain how that is going to be accomplished, but I'm beginning to think more about it. I know I will be more understanding and compassionate. I have to stop there for now. Still, I'm trying to find my way. Trying to get on with life.

Even so, your ever-present absence just about does me in at times. A big part of my heart will always belong to you. But

I think the best way I can honor your memory is to continue to serve the Lord you loved in the best way I know how. So I have to get past dwelling on *my* loss and *my* grief and *my* hurt and *my* loneliness and *my* needs. There isn't much left after I muck through all those miles of *my*'s.

I listened to a love song on the radio today, and I didn't cry. Instead, this incredibly peaceful feeling of gratefulness to God for what we had and how wonderful it was overwhelmed me. I was awash in the memory of your love for me instead of the pain of losing you. It was a wonderful feeling.

Of course, I realize this moment of growth may have been only a flicker, and I will probably still have those moments of complete abandonment when I blubber at your grave. Yet somehow, I think I have taken a tiny step forward.

I still wish you hadn't left me alone. I still wish for what we had and for companionship. But there's a tiny, infinitesimal part of me that is willing to accept how things are now, a part of me that senses that I really am going to be okay. Somehow I realize that my willingness doesn't mean I don't still adore you. It just means I'm beginning to learn the lesson God wants me to learn in this moment of time and space. Perhaps there is a sense that this is "momentary light affliction" after all. If I must remain under it, then I will. I can still accomplish a lot for God on my own. I'm beginning to be willing to do that. Does this mean I have achieved contentment?

HOW TO HELP

LISTEN

Sometimes I just need to talk things out.

If my reasoning falters along the way,

you don't always have to correct it.

Time will likely do that,

and I have plenty of time.

For now, just listen.

HOW IT FEELS

Yesterday the meaning of active obedience became clearer to me. I was alone in the house — a rather unusual occurrence. I had cloistered myself at home, committed to doing some file sorting and rearranging of my office space. The sorting part of the task included the last box of things from my dead husband's office and some other personal things of his that needed organizing and packing for safekeeping.

The lid came off the box, revealing items from his office desk. Shoe polish and a brush. Toothpaste. Mouthwash. Dental floss. I had a fleeting wish that scientists could take the DNA off the toothbrush and create a new husband for me. There were other things too — paper from work that no longer had meaning, meeting minutes, the mouse pad with the football players on it.

After a few hours of sorting and remembering, I felt I had done well. I cried, but I didn't rage against the realities represented by the box of no-longer-needed stuff. I went downstairs for a break, made coffee, took up the novel I am reading, and sat down at my kitchen table. The silence in the house descended, but it was not ominous, and it was not something I felt a need to fill. For the first time in a long time, the silence was friendly.

Gazing across the room above the fireplace where an oil

painting we always called *The Lion of the Tribe of Judah* hangs, I was reminded of Christ's presence, even in my seemingly empty house. It was as if He Himself were nudging me, asking me if I would accept the reality of the present. Would I trust Him with it . . . and would I say yes to an unknown future?

I sat for a moment, looking around me. The dog was asleep at my feet, and my book was open. It was a good book, and I was enjoying a good cup of coffee and the chance to put up my feet and know that I had done well that day. And for just a brief moment, I was able by God's grace to think, *If this is the future for me, Lord . . . if this is what You want . . . then I will myself to say yes to an empty house.*

It was only the briefest moment of obedience. But its impact has remained with me, even in the moments when I find myself less willing to contemplate emptiness and more fearful — again — of the future. I'm going to try something new. In the moments when I am tempted to look into the future and panic, I'm going to exercise my will to say yes. Even when it is against everything my heart and mind are screaming, I am going to say yes to the Father. I gave Him my heart long ago. Now I'm going to give Him my broken dreams. I picture myself picking up the pieces one by one, laying them in His hands, and whispering, "Yes, Father. Yes."

It's a beginning.

HOW TO HELP

ENCOURAGE ME

If you see signs of progress, let me know.

Tell me it's good to see me smile.

Tell me it's good to hear me laugh.

Sometimes I'm tempted to feel guilty

about being happy.

Encourage me.

༼ིཏ྅

BE PREPARED FOR THE REBOUND

Recovery isn't a straight line.

Don't expect it to be.

༼ིཏ྅

HANG IN THERE

Don't let go.

HOW IT FEELS

What, I have wondered of late, does one do with the rest of one's life? The part *after*. It has taken me two years to realize that my life's greatest moments are, quite likely, behind me. There were smaller great moments leading up to the greatest. Small victories over death and anger and fear and all of those things that challenge everyone facing terminal illness. We triumphed fairly well over them. My personal best was that Saturday morning when I lay next to him on the bed and coached him into heaven while our children watched. I was not hysterical. I was not anything I should not be.

Everything has been downhill since then.

Sometimes I have had a sense of waiting, still, for the next thing to arrive that will require me to ante up and deliver. To show what I am made of. To *live my faith*.

But I don't think there's much of anything left that could require so much from me. The angels probably watched in amazement on that day two years ago. Since then, there hasn't been much in my life to interest them. Or me.

My finest hour is behind me. The next thirty years or so are the *after*. This realization has left me feeling hollow. I am going through the motions of living, but I am not alive. It's different from the widows who don't want to live after their mates die. I want to keep on living. I want to love someone again. I want to be loved. In every sense of these words, I mean it.

But my finest hours are in the past. I am simply a holdover from a better time, someone going through the motions and doing my part to keep my little corner of the world percolating in a mildly interesting way. And watching others face their finest hours and remembering what that was like and trying to help them through and along the way into their *after*.

I hate this part.

Dear "Only One," I need you. I thought I would be all right, but I am not all right at all. I don't know what to do about so many things. You always knew what to do, and if you didn't, we decided together. And now I don't have anyone. I wish I could see you again and ask you what to do.

Those last months hurt me so much when you pulled away and headed toward heaven, but that pain was nothing compared to the emptiness I feel now.

I have to learn to be content with this, but I don't know how. How can I be content with empty arms?

I miss you. If I wrote those words all day every day for the rest of my life, it wouldn't be enough to express how much I miss you.

I don't know how to *be* without you.

HOW TO HELP

CELEBRATE LIFE
If you appreciate life more because
of my loss, tell me.
It helps me to know that something good is coming
from all this hurt.

PRAY FOR ME
Because the second year is turning out to be harder than the first.

PRAY FOR ME
You don't even need to send a card to tell me you're doing it.

PRAY FOR ME
Every time you think of me.

PRAY FOR ME
Every time you think of my children.

PRAY FOR ME

On Sunday when I am sitting alone in church.

PRAY FOR ME

On Monday when I am starting another week alone.

PRAY FOR ME

On Tuesday when the week stretches everlastingly before me.

PRAY FOR ME

On Wednesday when I've made it through two days but don't
think I can do a third.

PRAY FOR ME

On Thursday when I begin to dread the weekend.

PRAY FOR ME

On Friday night when I don't want to do anything but also don't
want to be home alone.

PRAY FOR ME

On Saturday when everyone else is spending time with family.

PRAY FOR ME

On Sunday when I am sitting alone in church.

PRAY FOR ME

When it's been long enough that you think I should be
all right by now.

PRAY FOR ME

Pray.

Pray.

My future used to be volumes, but now it is a blank page.

In closing . . .
a word about closure

My oldest son's best friend was killed when the boys were four years old. His mother cried when my son graduated from high school over a dozen years later. She has two healthy, wonderful children and a good life. But grief for the loss of her firstborn son returns with the milestones she will never share with him. It would not surprise me at all if she sheds a tear when my son's first son is born — grief for the grandchildren she will not have from that beloved son, no less beloved because he left us when he was only four years old. No other child can fill the Thomas-sized hole in that mother's heart.

My best friend died in 1996. Just this past year when I was on my hands and knees scrubbing the toilet in what used to be *her* bathroom (and is now the bathroom at my writing studio because I married her widowed husband), I cried. The last time I scrubbed this toilet, my best friend was dying in the other room. I wish she were here. I wish she hadn't died. I wish . . .

My new husband found me crying and understood. (We

laughed, then, about how convoluted life can be and how, if I still had my best friend Celest, there would be more than just a slight problem with my having this new husband.) I have a new best friend. But she is not Celest. The Celest-sized hole in my life remains.

I am remarried. Life is good. But my love for my new husband has neither replaced nor diminished my love for Robert Thomas Whitson. I wish he could be here to talk late at night with his sons, to teach Sunday school classes, to give the Elders' reports that always included humor and made the congregation laugh, to cheer on the Huskers football team. When our first grandchild is born, I know I will cry because I am crying even now as I write this. God has given me new love for a new mate. But it is new love. The old love remains. No one will ever fill the Robert-sized hole in my life.

Jesus promised His followers that His burdens are light, and I have been in grief long enough to experience His lightening of my load. But it is a *lightening*, not a removal. The emotions of loss are still there just on the other side of today. Sometimes those emotions punch open the door between the past and the present, march into my life, and remind me of what I have lost.

We do not close the door on people who have changed our lives forever. We celebrate what they have meant to us, and we look forward to seeing them again. And sometimes, even decades later, we cry.

So in the closing of this book on grief, I want to say that closure, in the way most people mean it, does not exist. We gain new friends, we have more children, we remarry. The pain of loss becomes less, and we learn to live around it. But we still carry it. Sometimes it returns in full force, and we find ourselves crying years after everyone around us assumes we have accomplished what our culture calls closure. This is painful, but it is not necessarily a bad thing. I think it is part of being human. It is part of loving and being loved. And yes, it is worth it.

after a while

After a while you learn the subtle difference
  between holding a hand and chaining a soul
And you learn that love doesn't mean leaning
  and company doesn't always mean security
And you begin to learn that kisses aren't contracts
  and presents aren't promises
And you begin to accept your defeats
  with your head up and your eyes ahead
  with the grace of a woman, not the grief of a child
And you learn to build all your roads on today
  because tomorrow's ground is too uncertain for plans
  and futures have a way of falling down in mid-flight.
After a while you learn that even sunshine burns
  if you get too much.
So you plant your own garden and decorate your own soul
  instead of waiting for someone to bring you flowers.

And you learn that you really can endure

      that you really are strong

      and you really do have worth

And you learn and you learn

      with every goodbye you learn . . .

VERONICA A. SHOFFSTALL

aBOUT THE aUTHOR

A native of southern Illinois, Stephanie Grace Whitson Higgins has resided in Nebraska since 1975. While teaching her four homeschooled children their state history unit, she became interested in the lives of the women who settled her adopted state. What Stephanie likes to call "playing with imaginary friends" eventually became her first novel, *Walks the Fire*, published in 1995. Stephanie's books have not only appeared on the ECPA Bestsellers List but have also been finalists for the Christy Award and the Inspirational Readers' Choice Award. An avid quilter and student of antique quilts, Stephanie volunteers for the International Quilt Study at the University of Nebraska — Lincoln, where she has been guest curator and lecturer.

In 1996, Stephanie lost her best friend to cancer three days after her own husband was diagnosed with an incurable form of non-Hodgkin's lymphoma. Later that same year, her mother and father died within six weeks of each other. Thus, 1996 marked the beginning of the grief journey that has resulted in *How to*

Help a Grieving Friend: A Candid Guide for Those Who Care.

Widowed in 2001, Stephanie developed a full-time writing and speaking ministry. She and her new husband and blended family live in Lincoln, Nebraska, where they are active in their local Bible teaching church. To read excerpts from her books or to learn more, visit her at www.stephaniegracewhitson.com.

MORE WORDS OF HOPE AND ENCOURAGEMENT.

The Power of a Friend

The Power of a Friend highlights essential biblical passages on friendship in the easy-to-read language of *The Message*.

Eugene H. Peterson 1-57683-723-8

The Power of a Prayer

Celebrate the power of communicating with God through *The Power of a Prayer*, featuring the easy-to-read language of *The Message*.

Eugene H. Peterson 1-57683-722-X

Friendship Counseling

To help people in pain, try friendship counseling. This approach offers "life words"—words that sensitively point strugglers toward building character and drawing closer to God.

Kevin D. Huggins, Ph.D. 1-57683-299-6

To order copies, visit your local Christian bookstore,
call NavPress at 1-800-366-7788, or log on to www.navpress.com.
To locate a Christian bookstore near you,
call 1-800-991-7747.

NAVPRESS ®
BRINGING TRUTH TO LIFE
www.navpress.com